Let us survive
Inside a sacred space.
Look at the Earth.
She feels us. She feeds us.

Look to the West.
Look to the North.
Look to the East.
Look to the South.

Look at the Sky.
He feeds us. He heals us.
Inside a sacred space
Let us survive.

Star Quilt

Poems by
Roberta Hill Whiteman

Foreword by Carolyn Forché

Illustrations by Ernest Whiteman

Holy Cow! Press   •   MINNEAPOLIS   •   1984

Acknowledgment is made to the following magazines and anthologies in which some of these poems first appeared:

The American Poetry Review: "A Nation Wrapped in Stone," "Beginning the Year at Rosebud, S.D.," "Direction," "Dream of Rebirth," "Lines for Marking Time"
Carriers of the Dream Wheel: "Midnight on Front Street"
First Skin Around Me: Contemporary American Tribal Poetry: "The Recognition"
The Nation: "Midwinter Stars"
The North American Review: "Patterns"
The Northwest Review: "Falling Moon"
Poetry Northwest: "Star Quilt"
The Southern Review: "Seal at Stinson Beach"
The Stream Invents a Smile: "Made of Mist"
Sun Tracks: "An Old Man's Round for the Geese," "Song for Facing Winter"
The Third Woman: Third World Women Writers in America: "Leap in the Dark"
Voices of the Rainbow: "Winter Burn"
Where We Are: A Montana Poets Anthology: "Blue Mountain"
Wisconsin Academy Review: "Currents," "Variations for Two Voices"

ISBN 0-930100-16-6 (cloth)
ISBN 0-930100-17-4 (paper)

Library of Congress Number: 83-080591

Photograph of Roberta Hill Whiteman by Ernest Whiteman

Cover illustration and all illustrations © 1984 by Ernest Whiteman

Second Printing, 1985

Printed in the United States of America

Publisher's Address:

Holy Cow! Press
Post Office Box 618
Minneapolis, Minnesota 55440

This project is supported by a grant from the National Endowment for the Arts in Washington, D.C., a Federal agency.

In Memory of Our Parents
John Atlee and Eva Mae Whiteman
and
Charles Allen and Eleanor Smith Hill

TABLE OF CONTENTS

FOREWORD

Winter, 1976. In an anthology of contemporary Native American poetry (*Carriers of the Dream Wheel*) I came upon the work of Roberta Hill Whiteman and began my search for her. It was my hope that she would agree to a reading in California, blessing my students and all others in attendance with a voice *like straw on fire*. Here was a woman poet who would be *apprentice to the blood / in spite of the mood of the world*. She was living in Rosebud, South Dakota, then and on the day of her anticipated performance, a blizzard kept her there. We were not to meet for five more years.

Now each of us must suffer / his own spirit she writes, and in the intervening years the poems of "Star Quilt" were completed. The vision is luminous: the particularity of lit tubes in an old radio seen as a *shimmering city*, the breadth of one who, *as if without a history*, would *always walk / the cluttered streets of this hapless continent*. One finds in this work a map of the journey each of us must complete, wittingly or not, as children and exiles of the Americas. So there is spiritual guidance here, uncommon in contemporary letters. I have long admired Roberta Hill Whiteman and celebrate that, with this book, her poems have become more possible in this country.

Carolyn Forché
December, 1983

STAR QUILT

These are notes to lightning in my bedroom.
A star forged from linen thread and patches.
Purple, yellow, red like diamond suckers, children

of the star gleam on sweaty nights. The quilt unfolds
against sheets, moving, warm clouds of Chinook.
It covers my cuts, my red birch clusters under pine.

Under it your mouth begins a legend,
and wide as the plain, I hope Wisconsin marshes
promise your caress. The candle locks

us in forest smells, your cheek tattered
by shadow. Sweetened by wings, my mothlike heart
flies nightly among geraniums.

We know of land that looks lonely,
but isn't, of beef with hides of velveteen,
of sorrow, an eddy in blood.

Star quilt, sewn from dawn light by fingers
of flint, take away those touches
meant for noisier skins,

anoint us with grass and twilight air,
so we may embrace, two bitter roots
pushing back into the dust.

I. Sometimes in Other Autumns

DIRECTION

Walk east. Dawn polishes the sky,
turning frost to rainbows, vapor.
A fever, alien and wild, is in me,
like slivers, cut loose from the sun's core,
flow in my fingers, ease in my eyes.
The sun leaves light under trees,
circle on circle, drop on drop. Pine moths
suckle daisies to light up mountain slopes.

I saw your picture, and let aches surrender
to the avalanche. This place holds the memory
of rocking. Slow, white curtains breathe in gusts.
Flowery songs hummed lazily out of tune.
The sky changed; I've become a stranger
hating sloven clocks and vacant pain.

In the south, heat lashes you to cherries. I chronicle
the sun as it burns jewel-like reflections between leaves,
as it flares into air this wavering smell of camomile.
Smoke drifts along peonies, wet, ant-seeded,
and rests in lilacs rubbed with blue sky. I would be content
as a gull watching waves bend light into dark.

In the threshing wind, a gate swings.
Bones were never meant for one like her. Terrible red eye
at every door step. Circled sunlight
cups the trees. A misty heron flies along the pine;
she's the reason I've come. Mountains hush
my dull senses, hush the deep-throated ache, the uneasy trees.

A father is cigarette smoke late on winter nights,
tears on a weather-tender face,
a smell of earth and powder.
The piano and violin lonely, and the artist gone,
she slipped into the blue painting,
where a dwarf hides in the clouds.

Like you, I wait first light to strike
darkness. In north air, the mazes twist repeatedly,
perfection never rests. To find a lost tradition,
I would watch your heart for signs,
cracklings in a pine,
footsteps on a marsh floor.

Our closets held the scent of loss,
and clothes for a woman no longer needy.
But the rocking I hold true,
though it often robs my heart.
The rocks from the man in the French Sudan,
the quartz and mica dissolved with kaleidoscopes.
Snow patterns in red and blue,
broken into, scattered on a rug,
like stories for a child's idle years.

The moon leans west. Blurred by trees, she clings
to grey rock and grass in patches.
Small long cloud slung over a low mountain.
Dreams gather in these mists. I've lived
as a misshapen thing, bound by water and geese
in flight. Lights flicker up hard against bald stone.
No music lilts my stifling home. I live here
unafraid of storms. No music, just rain,
this thunder, growing.

LINES FOR MARKING TIME

Women know how to wait here.
They smell dust on wind and know you haven't come.
I've grown lean, walking along dirt roads,
under a glassy sun, whispering to steps.
Twenty years I've lived on ruin. When I escaped,
they buried you. All that's left is a radio
with a golden band. It smells of heat,
old baseball games, a shimmering city inside.
The front door has stopped banging and the apple tree
holds an old tire strange children swing in.

This house with broken light has lost me
now, when the sweet grass dries. Its scent lingers
in the living room among sewing and worn-out shoes.
In your silence, I grew visions for myself, and received
a name no one could live up to. Blood rises
on hot summer wind, rose petals trickle
past rough solemn wood. Hear the distant sobbing?
An Indian who's afraid of tears. She charms her eyes
into smiling, waits for the new blue star. Answers
never come late.

Look west long enough, the moon will grow
inside you. Coyote hears her song; he'll teach you now.
Mirrors follow trails of blood and lightning.
Mother needs the strength of one like you. Let blood
dry, but seize the lightning. Hold it like your mother
rocks the trees. In your fear, watch the road, breathe deeply.
Indians know how to wait.

MIDNIGHT ON FRONT STREET

"Peacock colored tears and rotten oranges,"
said the fire. "You swim in salt and think
it is the sea." Thief, webs like crowns keep us
near this door. You laugh. One hundred voices answer,
"No migration." You act the warrior, wind thief,
yet watchers from shade declare your sky stormless.
By whose right do you court exhausting thunder
bound in leaves?
Whose night rocks do you drown like mossy turtles?
I shelter with claws one final whisper:
Ashes for a tired moon.

Once Mosquito sang in swamps
on the far moon rim. Green flanks bridged the silence
with music. A thief hidden in the clouds
hacked his tail and a sea sound thundered,
hacked his wings and the rustling trees broke,
smashed his flanks and the silent dust boiled
into mountain, forest. Birds flooded from his head.
Animals ran from mouth or ear. Shells cracked
and each became a man of granite. Each a nation.
The fire steams and spits. Looking skyward, I feel
my fingers curl.

The eaglebone cries. My lair mushrooms.
Seven echoes fell the walls. Across glaring fields,
light sweeps in a rush of stars. Notes burn
on an empty rise. In Wyoming,
she howled and dark plains drank up rainbows.
I rub my arms with magic stones,
call nets down, down into mud,
and hunt for other thieves. My rooms fill with frost
and snarled roots. Haze around a streetlight grows.
I must wait. In the mirror a woman
is answering sleep. Elms bend against the night.

UNDERGROUND WATER

"When spirit is heavy, it turns to water . . ."
                    Carl Jung

A child, awaking, takes the long way home.
Rain glistens on the window.
He hears voices abandoning weather. Narrow streams
trickle in the dark between streetlights
and a cloud folds down like a rag.
Down gutters, a dark field waits his escape.
There, birds flutter in the wet leaves
while clover blooms like the only stars.
A smell of mud skims through the room,
tired perfume on a blush of air.
A cat in heat asks its question
and tap water thumps its way alone.
As he walks by, the dresser creaks
and swirls of paint sigh like night blooming dahlias.
Cabbage moths dancing against his chin,
he pads to his parents' bed and crawls between them.
The sound of underground water rustles
like taffeta around their hips. It pulls him
toward the warmth of sea plums.
A birthmark of foam encircles his neck.
Listening in the quilted dark,
he slips away to another sun. From there,
he watches mother stare at a smoky bulb
in this last room. She'll never hear
the lilies rise, the weeds spin in the shallows
or water lap the half-awakened stones.
She hasn't words enough to lock his days.
They say goodbye on every heartbeat.
At every moment, dozens of waterbirds
whir in flight, their quicksilver wings
confusing the leaves. Goodbye,
goodbye, the curtains breathe,

while memories, those stains on linen, remain
the last design. With bones of moonlight,
she skirts the water's edge. On her head,
a cap of fluttering voices. Cabbage moths,
her mad soul's journeymen, play in her hair.
Turning in her sleep, she feels again his breath
upon her cheek. Softer than the eye closing in death,
a curled leaf falls from his forehead
and is lost in the grass.

CURRENTS

How differently the river gleams
now you are gone.
Once it rushed headlong
down the plain,
polishing the canyon stone
until the fluted edges
filled with fire,
but now two currents churn,
converging in a single ripple
that never reaches shore.
Like a diamondback
migrating to mountains,
the ripple culls the current;
the far half jumps with light,
sending all shadow
back along the ridge,
while the other is subdued,
measuring an obscure song,
deep as plunder, doubly lost.

Some said you were unhappy,
that you had planned
to travel tomorrow.
Tomorrow. The right cadence,
the right words are wedged
in the hoof of the horse
that took you
beyond the clatter of dishes
and toys, beyond the market
bartering rifles,
beyond broken glass
or the need for shoes.
I believe your beloved
rode that dark stallion,
so much like the one

he owned before the war.
At last he came to carry you
over the dim shimmer of mountains,
along the white road
into the smoke of stars.

Worlds upon worlds
the stallion restored
you to your beloved.
We couldn't call you back,
lovely autumn mother
with a face so like the moon.
Please look once again,
for at last we're learning
to live as you have taught,
taking time to love each day,
to live without regret.
Now each of us must suffer
his own spirit,
and catch the starlight
aging in his hands.
Now each of us knows the river
will never be the same,
and sometimes it gets hard
to see the undiscovered depth,
or to hear the wind
singing above our cries.

In memory of Eva Whiteman

Leap in the Dark

"The experience of truth is indispensible
for the experience of beauty and the sense
of beauty is guided by a leap in the dark."
        Arthur Koestler

I.

Stoplights edged the licorice street with ribbon,
neon embroidering wet sidewalks. She turned

into the driveway and leaped in the dark. A blackbird
perched on the bouncing twig of a maple, heard

her whisper, "Stranger, lover, the lost days are over.
While I walk from car to door, something inward opens

like four o'clocks in rain. Earth, cold from autumn,
pulls me. I can't breathe the same

with dirt for marrow and mist for skin,
blurring my vision, my vision's separate self.

I stand drunk in this glitter, under the sky's grey shelter.
The city maple, not half so bitter, hurls itself

in two directions, until both tips darken and disappear,
as I darken my reflection in the smoking mirror

of my home. How faint the sound of dry leaves,
like the clattering keys of another morning, another world."

II.

She looked out the window at some inward greying door.
The maple held her glance, made ground fog from her cigarette.

Beyond uneven stairs, children screamed,
gunned each other down. Then she sealed her nimble dreams

with water from a murky bay. "For him I map
this galaxy of dust that turns without an answer.

When it rains, I remember his face in the corridor
of a past apartment and trace the anguish around his mouth,

his wrinkled forehead, unguarded eyes, the foreign fruit
of an intricate sadness. With the grace that remains,

I catch a glint around a door I cannot enter.
The clock echoes in dishtowels; I search love's center

and bang pans against the rubble of my day, the lucid
grandeur of wet ground, the strangeness of a fatal sun

that makes us mark on the margin of our loss,
trust in the gossamer of touch, trust in the late-plowed field."

III.

When the sun opened clouds and walked into her mongrel soul,
she chopped celery into rocky remnants of the sea,

and heard fat sing up bread, a better dying.
The magnet in each seed of the green pepper kept her flying,

floating toward memories that throb like clustered stars:
the dark water laughter of ducks, a tangle of November oaks,

toward sudden music on a wheel of brilliant dust
where like a moon she must leap back and forth

from emptiness. "I remember the moon shimmering
loss and discovery along a water edge, and skirting

a slice of carrot, I welcome eternity in that sad eye of autumn.
Rare and real, I dance while vegetables sing in pairs.

I hug my death, my chorus of years, and search
and stretch and leap, for I will be apprentice to the blood

in spite of the mood of a world
that keeps rusting, rusting the wild throats of birds."

IV.

In lamplight she saw the smoke of another's dream:
her daughter walk woods where snow weighs down pine,

her son cry on a bridge that ends in deep-rooted dark,
her man, stalled on a lonely road, realize his torque

was alcohol and hatred. "Hungry for silence, I listen
to wind, to the sound of water running down mountain,

my own raw breath. Between the sounds, a seaborn god
plays his reed in the caverns of my being.

I wear his amethyst, let go my dreams: Millars, Lacewings,
and Junebugs scatter, widen and batter the dark,

brightening this loud dust with the fever of their eyes.
Oh crazy itch that grabs us beyond loss

and lets us forgive, so that we can answer birds and deer,
lightning and rain, shadow and hurricane.

Truth waits in the creek, cutting the winter brown hills.
It sings with needles of ice, sings because of its scar."

In the Longhouse, Oneida Museum

House of five fires, you never raised me.
Those nights when the throat of the furnace
wheezed and rattled its regular death,
I wanted your wide door,

your mottled air of bark and working sunlight,
wanted your smokehole with its stars,
and your roof curving its singing mouth above me.
Here are the tiers once filled with sleepers,

and their low laughter measured harmony or strife.
Here I could wake amazed at winter,
my breath in the draft a chain of violets.
The house I left as a child now seems

a shell of sobs. Each year I dream it sinister
and dig in my heels to keep out the intruder
banging at the back door. My eyes burn
from cat urine under the basement stairs

and the hall reveals a nameless hunger,
as if without a history, I should always walk
the cluttered streets of this hapless continent.
Thinking it best I be wanderer,

I rode whatever river, ignoring every zigzag,
every spin. I've been a fragment, less than my name,
shaking in a solitary landscape,
like the last burnt leaf on an oak.

What autumn wind told me you'd be waiting?
House of five fires, they take you for a tomb,
but I know better. When desolation comes,
I'll hide your ridgepole in my spine

and melt into crow call, reminding my children
that spiders near your door
joined all the reddening blades of grass
without oil, hasp or uranium.

ELEGY FOR JIM WHITE

You must have said 'yes' this time,
yes to squeaks tucked in hotel rooms,
yes to rainwater trembling in the gutter,
yes to Aldebaran under clouds.

I thought I'd always find you here,
sitting at the breakfast table
while the notes of a distant dove
eased the shadow in your heart.

But when the poem rose from the page
and drifted toward eternity, you gazed
at your hand as it learned dexterity
from sunlight. You held the wings of dahlias.

All our imperfections remain.
They were your wealth. In your view,
the mold played equal to the night.
Once you said you were afraid

that dying meant no more birds,
no mud, no buses bouncing their patrons,
no sidewalks steaming in mid-July.
How right you were, my friend.

Although dying's never new,
your loss has worked a different world
where planets shape a sickle before dawn.
As Cassiopeia rocks to sleep, a husband

down the street drives home
in time to bleed. Underneath the sidewalk,
one fickle ant broods about last summer.
Since your death, the snow

carries more than she can name.
I wrap the wind inside my coat.
My blood blazes like a crystal.
May all these imperfections remain.

NETT LAKE, MINNESOTA

for Minoka

The only sunlight left bleaches aspens
far across the lake where they rise like a shout
above the grey hoods of pine. Down at my feet,
ripples unravel every reflection
into glyphs, all shifting form. Loss,
loss, lost. The constant resonance brings hope
that colors grow richer in loneliness,
yet with this rain, autumn fades to embers,
folding layer after layer
of scarlet into auburn, magenta into slate.
Covering the shore, the long leaves of rice
wave eastward, inventing shadows that flicker
all at once, as if hidden dancers
tug each other's arm and scatter
before my unaccustomed eyes.

Ducks swing a low arc around Spirit Island,
covered with clouds in a variety of greys,
some with bright borders, some massed together
like a pile of dowdy nightgowns.
A slit in the lifting fog lengthens to reveal
an oak shimmering with the yellow wings of warblers,
a bit of truth fanned from a darkened coal.
The people say rocks out there
carry the clearest words. Spirits live
inside the caves, unafraid of dark-lipped water
or this turning time. Those who wait for dawn
wait with them. Hush, hush, hushed.
The oak still holds its cache of fire.

I'll wrap four strands of hair
around a notch of the nearest pine.

A spider's web, come Spring.

II. "... Fighting back the Cold with Tongues"
—Richard Hugo

A Nation Wrapped in Stone

for Susan Iron Shell

When night shadows slipped across the plain, I saw a man
beside his horse, sleeping where neither man nor horse
had been. I've prayed
to a star that lied. The spirits near the ceiling of your room,
did they leave on horseback, turning dew into threads
by moonlight?
In wild stretch of days, you didn't fear ashes or weeping.
We, left behind, can't warm sunlight.
Isaac, you left with the wind.

The chokecherry grows slower. I held your trembling wife,
and windows trembled in our north room. The creek gnaws
remaining snow. Our blood runs pale.
You taught us to be kind to one another. Now we wake, questioning
our dreams. Nighthawks in warm fog. A nation wrapped in stone.
What do nurses
know of hay, of scents that float broken between canyons,
of strength in a worn face? You wept love, not death.
Around your bed, owls stood.

The north wind hunts us with music, enough pain
to set fires in ancient hills. West winds growl
around Parmelee.
The tanned, uneven banks will hold more frost. Unlike dust,
we cannot die from tears. You've settled
on a quiet prairie. Shrouded eyes
in thickets give a reason to contain
this heavy rind. We are left with grief, sinking boneward,
and time to watch rain soak the trees.

REACHING YELLOW RIVER

"It isn't a game for girls,"
he said, grabbing a fifth
with his right hand,
the wind with his left.

"For six days
I raced Jack Daniels.
He cheated, told jokes.
Some weren't even funny.

That's how come he won.
It took a long time
to reach this Yellow River.
I'm not yet thirty,

or is it thirty-one?
Figured all my years
carried the same hard thaw.
Out here, houselights hid

deep inside the trees.
For awhile I believed this road
cut across to Spring Creek
and I was trucking home.

I could kid you now,
say I ran it clean,
gasping on one lung,
loaded by a knapsack

of distrust and hesitation.
I never got the tone
in all the talk of cure.
I sang Honor Songs, crawled

the railroad bridge to Canada.
Dizzy from the ties,
I hung between both worlds.
Clans of blackbirds circled

the nearby maple trees.
The dark heart of me said
no days more than these.
As sundown kindled the sumacs,

stunned by the river's smile,
I had no need for heat,
no need to feel ashamed.
Inside me then the sound

of burning leaves. Tell them
I tumbled through a gap on the horizon.
No, say I stumbled through a hummock
and fell in a pit of stars.

When rain weakened my stride,
I heard them singing
in a burl of white ash,
took a few more days to rave

at them in this wood.
Then their appaloosas nickered
in the dawn and they came
riding down a close ravine.

Though the bottle was empty,
I still hung on. Foxtails beat
the grimace from my brow
until I took off my pain

like a pair of old boots.
I became a hollow horn filled
with rain, reflecting everything.
The wind in my hand

burned cold as hoarfrost
when my grandfather nudged me
and called out
my Lakota name."

. . .

*In memory of Mato Heholgeca's
grandson*

OVERCAST DAWN

This morning I feel dreams dying.
One trace is this feather
fallen from a gull,
with its broken shaft,
slight white down,
and long dark tip
that won't hold air.
How will you reach me
if all our dreams are dead?
Will I find myself
as empty as an image,
that death mask of a woman
reflected in car windows?
Help me, for every bird
remembers as it preens
the dream that lifted
it to flight.
Help me, for the sky
is close with feathers,
falling today
from sullen clouds.

Beginning the Year at Rosebud, S.D.

No pavement chalks the plain with memories,
rows of curb crumbling to dirt each twilight.
Raw bones bend from an amber flood of gravel,
used clothing, whiskey. We walked, and a dead dog
seemed to leap from an iced shore, barks swelling her belly.
Three days I've waited, eyes frosted shut
to illusions of scrap and promising wind.

I'm untrapped here, in another place where the banister
interned my smile and glued my soul to the lion's mane,
walls nibble this new year. While cedar cradles
its medicine in ironing, I see my father's red eyes lock
thunder in the living room. Someone's brain cries in the basket,
watches steam and church bells fade. My empty hands ache
from stains and cigarette smoke. I am a renegade,
name frozen at birth, entrails layered with scorpions.

Hay fields have poisoned my ears by now.
The fourth day grows heavy and fat like an orchid.
A withered grandmother's face trickles wisdom
of buffalo wallows and graveyards marked
with clumps of sage. Here, stars are ringed
by bitter wind and silence. I know of a lodestone in the prairie,
where children are unconsoled by wishes,
where tears salt bread.

Winter Burn

When birds break open the sky, a smell of snow
blossoms on the wind. You sleep, wrapped up
in blue dim light, like a distant leaf of sage.
I drink the shadow under your car
and rise, clumsy, glazed with cold.
Sun, gleaming in frost, reach me.
Touch through the window this seed that longs
little by little to flare up orange and sing.
Branches turn to threads against the sun.
Help us to wake up, enormous space that makes
us waver, dark horizon that keeps us strong.

Your heart pours over this land, pours over memories
of wild plum groves,
laughter, a blur between leaves.
These fences hold back frost, let horses run.
Spirits hunt our human warmth
in these quiet rooms. Dogs follow us,
bark at the piercing air. I sort beans,
wish for something neither key nor hand can give.
I must watch you suffering the doubt and grace
of foxes. Let clear winter burn away my eyes.
Let this seed amaze the ground again.

Beside barrels, a mouse glares at me,
folding against the present like a draft against a flame.
Curious bitter eyes tick away
my years. Women have always heard this,
his rattle signaling a day brought wide
like slow ripples in a river.
Ask him why water drifts over moss.
Your hair grows fish-haunted. You are never warned.
Ask why those waving weeds steal what you become.
His answer, the slow tick of fire.
Near timber, axes sing inside the poles.

You chop wood and chop a buried city
from your bones. Far off, the clouds are floating into dusk.
We stack up logs traveling to the dry field
of our breath. Like ants, we pace the ground,
and let a strange heat shake our darkness,
an old web streams through the door.
Hushed steps follow you to valleys,
where, aching and ringing, you no longer want to look,
until, touching the sudden pulse of all we are,
you burn into the yellow grass of winter,
into one reed, trembling on the plain.

MIDWINTER STARS

The trees across the street have loved me
in your absence. The Pole star, caught by branches
of the front yard elm, blurs
when I look at it directly and passes
through midwinter slower than other stars.
Whenever you came by, the forest

filled with signs. A pocket in soft grass
meant resting deer. Hoofprints in the sand
lead through brush and fallen leaves
to even dimmer trails. I hated all my rooms.
The lonely light, absurd.
I warmed your shoulders one late November storm

and trees sang in minor chords.
Aware of dawn before it came, you woke,
smiled into clothes, juggled with coffee,
then drove away. I watched shadows turn
from indigo to grey.
Like other obsessions, this will change,

yet my arm was happy, numb
with all your weight. I learned the easy signs:
cloud cover, tracking snow.
I fell with every flake and wanted to drape
over trees, into city blocks, on those corners
where you bought beer, over cars and bridges

in that namesake of despair.
There are places I have never felt at ease,
where something taps against the glass,
the blackjack of a cop and bitter lives.
Who the hunter? Who the hunted? Who survives?
This cold circuit wobbles without rest.

I never could accept beginning or end.
You'll find on the other side of winter
crocus trembling in a bountiful dawn.
I plan to join the deer,
for in this dark, the trees bar my window
and not one shadow moves.

HORSES IN SNOW

They are a gift I have wanted again.
Wanted: One moment in mountains
when winter got so cold
the oil froze before it could burn.
I chopped ferns of hoarfrost from all the windows
and peered up at pines, a wedding cake
by a baker gone mad. Swirls by the thousand
shimmered above me until a cloud
lumbered over a ridge,
bringing the heavier white of more flurries.

I believed, I believed, I believed
it would last, that when you went out
to test the black ice or to dig out a Volkswagon
filled with rich women, you'd return
and we'd sputter like oil,
match after match, warm in the making.
Wisconsin's flat farmland never approved:
I hid in cornfields far into October,
listening to music that whirled from my thumbprint.
When sunset played havoc with bright leaves of alders,

I never mentioned longing or fear.
I crouched like a good refugee in brown creeks
and forgot why Autumn is harder than Spring.
But snug on the western slope of that mountain
I'd accept every terror, break open seals
to release love's headwaters to unhurried sunlight.
Weren't we Big Hearts? Through some trick of silver
we held one another, believing each motion the real one,
ah, lover, why were dark sources bundled up
in our eyes? Each owned an agate,

marbled with anguish, a heart or its echo,
we hardly knew. Lips touching lips,
did that break my horizon
as much as those horses broke my belief?
You drove off and I walked the old road,
scolding the doubles that wanted so much.
The chestnut mare whinnied a cloud into scrub pine.
In a windless corner of a corral,
four horses fit like puzzle pieces.
Their dark eyes and lashes defined by the white.

The colt kicked his hind, loped from the fence.
The mares and a stallion galloped behind,
lifting and leaping, finding each other
in full accord with the earth and their bodies.
No harm ever touched them once they cut loose,
snorting at flurries falling again.
How little our chances for feeling ourselves.
They vanished so quickly—one flick of a tail.
Where do their mountains and moments begin?
I stood a long time in sharpening wind.

SONG FOR FACING WINTER

for Mary, Christmas, 1976

Snug in your denims, you walk a wintry coast
counting how many gulls prefer the chill of purple tide.
Like you, the sea searches for a name.
When it recedes, a hint remains in bubbles
and in threaded sand. You skip down Fisherman's Wharf
through Chinatown, into the glitter and sell of Christmas.
Those women on the serious business of shopping,
with hands quick as recent history, don't stop
to consult the bears, stunned into miniature
by an artist of Cybis. Your guardians, glazed in brown,
have strayed from a northern forest to tell you
there'll be light enough for all your days.

Look sister, I give you sun rising through Spring haze.
Across that lake on a bluff of oak and pine, we'll hear
the cuckoo call. There the wind will sweep
in circles, twining shadow and shimmer
into a rope of dreams. Smell the air off the water,
the rice break new and clean against brown reeds.
Let's follow the grains of light down that watery road
toward mountains. Reminded of our riches, we could leap
and live again on the rim of northern hills.
Dad would sing the laughing song on that other shore,
so distant that death forgets the name.
We'll sway in time to cattails. They love the pulse of snow.

Your cigarette smoke rears like the red horse on Io
you spoke of in a poem. I've learned to love the dark from you,
the same insomnia of waiting, waiting for Dad
to slowly climb the stairs each bitter dawn,
waiting for a cocoon to fall from shoulders,
doomed and human. Like coals of February's fire,
we'll come to carry these substantial things: this lake

that ripples gently, this fog, the crow's return.
We'll welter on wind until the silence and the stillness
tell us we've been traveling since the birth of stars.
Let's take a step of simple joy. Let's play flute and sing,
watching with glad eyes star, snow and barren tree.

THE WHITE LAND

When Orion straddled his apex of sky,
over the white land we lingered loving.
The River Eridanus flickered, foretelling
tropical waves and birds arrayed
in feathers of sunset, but we didn't waste
that prickling dark.

Not a dog barked our arrival before dawn.
Only in sleep did I drift vagabond
and suffer the patterns that constantly state
time has no time. Fate is a warlord.
That morning I listened to your long breath
for decades.

That morning you said bears
fell over the white land. Leaving their lair
in thick polar fur, they roused our joy
by leaving no footprint. Fat ones fell headlong,
but most of them danced, then without quarrel,
balanced on branches.

I couldn't breathe in the roar of that plane,
flying me back to a wooded horizon.
Regular rhythms bridge my uneven sleep.
What if the wind in the white land keeps you?
The dishwater's luminous; a truck
grinds down the street.

I'UNI KWI ATHI? HIATHO.

White horses, tails high, rise from the cedar.
Smoke brings the fat crickets,
trembling breeze.
Find that holy place, a promise.
Embers glow like moon air.

I call you back from the grasses.
Wake me when sand pipers
fly. They fade,
and new sounds flutter. Cattails at sunrise.
Hair matted by sleep.

Sun on the meadow. Grey boughs lie tangled.
The ground I was born to
wants me to leave.
I've searched everywhere to tell you
my eyes are with the hazels.

Wind swells through fences, drones a flat ache for hours.
At night, music would echo
from your womanless bedroom.
Far down those bleaching cliffs,
roses shed a torrent.

Will you brush my ear? An ice bear sometimes lumbers west.
Your life still gleams, the edge melting.
I never let you know.
You showed me and how under snow and darkness,
the grasses breathe for miles.

III. Love, The Final Healer

THE RECOGNITION

We learn too late the useless way light leaves
footprints of its own. We traveled miles to Kilgore
in the submarine closeness of a car. Sand hills
recalling the sea. A coyote slipped across the road
before we knew. Night, the first skin around him.
He was coming from the river
where laughter calls out fish. Quietly a heavy wind
breaks against cedar. He doubled back,
curious, to meet the humming moons we rode
in this gully, without grass or stars. Our footprints
were foreign to him. He understood the light
and paused before the right front wheel, a shadow
of the mineral earth, pine air in his fur.
Such dogs avoid our eyes, yet he recognized and held
my gaze. A being both so terrible and shy
it made my blood desperate
for the space he lived in:
broad water cutting terraced canyons,
and ice gleaming under hawthorne like a floor of scales.
Thick river, remember we were light thanking light,
slow music rising. Trees perhaps, or my own voice
out of tune. I danced a human claim for him
in this gully. No stars. He slipped
by us, old as breath, moving in the rushing dark
like moonlight through tamarack,
wave on wave of unknown country.
Crazed, I can't get close enough
to this tumble wild and tangled miracle.
Night is the first skin around me.

STEPS

Digging earth from puddles she would wake stranded.
Hollyhocks flooded the back step. Morning grew bright
with leaves. In green schoolrooms, chalk bit blackboards.
Robins paced the blowing grass.
Picnic day, her father sat, muttering, "She's dead"
over and over to fresh rain,
his shoulders broken as her doll's.

The cow lay wrapped in drops like a bursting pear,
like micashist. Children ran through the ponds
under ferns. Its neck was a home for midges and its smell,
bleach for dingy clouds. In radiant sheets of water,
a shadow buried the sun.

Weeds grew to stone. She hid among witch hazels,
the yellow flowers, a tired beacon.
Night air flashed on empty fields.
Twice Minona teased their birth,
dotting the broken hay with footprints.
A flame danced through birches. Lights along the backbone.
Veins stuffed with stars. This life forbids comfort,
traces with fingers a terrible sharing. Years. Years to find
the right step.

Men stroked her thighs, tried to make her sleep.
Their throats went dry from calling, as ducks
caught in a thicket cry. Woolen mud never wakens,
yet bright maples gather pain.
Their sap glistens like beads in moon wash.

Pretend these mountains are not hungry.
I've heard a young voice
muttering at wind, like straw on fire.
She moves drunk toward the lightning,

letting her arms stiffen, wanting to be fog,
the smell of ripe fruit. I've covered her tracks
with a difficult river, and like a plover,
wade from water to rock and back. It foams beryl green
in the sunset, and at every bend, leaves something behind.

An Old Man's Round for the Geese

I know why the wild goose flies,
the blood in its veins is burning.
I know why the wild goose flies,
filled with incredible yearning.

He leaves magnolia, enchanted moss,
humming a song to the moon.
She leaves magnolia, enchanted moss,
looking for winter's neon.

They travel together dark above the trees.
I watch from the porch and long to go.
They travel together quiet as clouds,
I want wings that can bring more snow.

They flaunt their death, being blessed.
Oh rain, such clear nights are no more.
They taunt our death, being more alive.
Did we ever land facing wind from the shore?

They merge on a current one whistling night;
so close, the mist makes them a pair.
They merge on a current one whistling night
when bare branches break in green air.

May the stone throwers keep out the dark for them
and rhythms never rust in their veins.
May the stone throwers keep out the dark for us
until we emerge from our pain.

I wasn't as lucky as the geese
that meet to love a lifetime.
I wasn't as lucky as the geese.
Bring me more wine, more wine.

BLUE MOUNTAIN

for Richard Hugo

West of your door, Blue Mountain dreams of melting
to the sea. You wait a simple answer.
Tomorrow is a harvest.
I understand what roads you've climbed
in the tinted smoke of afternoon.
Crickets whir a rough sun into haze.
The thickly planted field invades your longing.

I left that mountain in easy goodbyes.
The moon flooding me home. The Garnet Range
like arms letting go moments
when too much talk grows fatal. Now
moss folds down in matted sleep. Watch
how wind burns lazily through maples.
I sweep and sweep these broken days to echoes.

More than land's between us. Wood smoke in the sun.
Timber shrinks below the bend.
Our walls stay thin. We trust them,
loving the light that bleeds around the shade.
Peepers show us why we live, astonished
at new frost. You taught me how to track
this ragged fire. Chickadees keep me going.

I've begged a place for you to come at last.
Clouds gather like mints. Warm, dancing like gnats
in sunshine, rain hugs your heavy arms. Your woman smiles.
The flint lake brightens. In the slow roll
of a wave, joy buries its weight deep
inside your lungs. One bird calls from a far-off pine.
You and Blue Mountain will reach the sea.

THE OLD WOMAN IN A SHOO

Hungry for a creek
with its churning full tilt tumble
down a rock-gutted wash,
she gathered the remnants of tears
in those puddles oil slicks had changed
into one dull hue.
Shaped like birds, they hang in oaks
at dawn while she talks openly
of loneliness before its shadow smothers her.
Children gone, she risks
its massive mouth, and I, the sifting
noise of a wrist on paper.

Hungry for an eagle flying
up from long pine toward solitude,
she crawled in bushes
next to an alley. Her heart
in a slipknot with no one to help her,
she let summer heat beg her blind.
Now the world grows upside-down,
becomes her heavy wings.
My children hear her singing
as they trudge to school.

FALLING MOON

Reach for arrows of falling light. A man once sang
in this temple. The moon stretched out
her richest dreams to him, softly touching
the faces of his people. Eyes of dark blood.
Hands like warm adobe.
Cedars drink thin air.
Ruins are left to us walking the paths of rain,
following where
shadows meet and listen.

They piled the even bricks to echo the moon's pale ring.
When she rose, whistling like a doe
in the quiet glare,
some would enter these dens, the deep rooms of wolves,
purer than we could wish,
without the weight of bodies.
What have we left? Secrets of dust and hate.
Below this rim world,
the earth fades like a prayer.

We wear stranger masks.
Seven miles from Porcupine
tanks chill the prairie. Flares bloom
in thunderheads to fall like flickering comets.
A boy crouches in dirt. He has held the sun.
Its hard gold fire breathes with him. Minneconjous fell
like snow. Sparkling water people.
Death will hum like ashes in their ears.
The stillness branches.

Deep inside the noise of burning comes
the sound of wings. When hawks die
singing, some hidden vein will burst inside my throat,
dreams will shiver on this haunted sleep.
Reach for arrows of rising light.

Bones flash like shells
in green salt grass.
A thin moon soars above the pines,
plants no blame in open fields.

I watch a weeping birch let its trail of leaves
ride a stalking wind.
Owls call thought the haze.
How can I mark this sorrow? We live the flames
of twilight. Dew claws drum the trappings of this dust.
Meeting canyons still hold blood and flesh.
Spirits rise on black-mouthed water, dance like grouse
in dry creek beds. Believe the distant ice,
the robber storm.

Inside the circled weeds, raw hours strike. Purple thistles
wrinkle near the corn.
Cottonwoods will answer
when they come to make the grey mare captive
in her flight.
I keep hearing singing in the sun.
It rustles through the turnips on those hills.
Crows will find us walking north.
You and I must gather under elms.

SCRAPS WORTHY OF WIND

I've walked those ruins and arranged
the ways I've died there
on scraps of paper worthy enough
for the wind. I've worked hard,
treading this lake that is my life,
floating with barely a breath
over the man-of-war's wave,
over these bubbles of death and departure.

In your letter you demanded I remember
the mirror I once shattered,
the tar from a street I fear. You taunt me
with losses I've mourned and put to rest.
You wrap them in innocent ribbons.
They wound with pink barbs.
Only one house remains
on the street where we played tag.

The witch still lives on the corner.
When she carries out the garbage, her hips stiffen
with pain. No one plays Dr. Rhodie in her yard,
finally degraded into tar and liquor store.
Does it matter rats, large as terriers,
crept down that alley, or that a woman
cried herself graveward,
longing for the wind of a bayou?

I'm that woman from whose mouth
a long white string of mucus
unwinds on a stair. We cannot hate
ourselves enough to justify
that world. I wore blame
until it became my birthmark,
but no more.
Death comes soon enough.

Already its mason has laid a mosaic
in my womb. In dreams I sweep
the floors of universities and make the dust
leap down their empty halls. That bleak air
will never hold my dancing.
Doctors peer and tear.
With one more slice, they will it gone.
Gone, but never done.

Waist deep in dying, at last I understand
nothing is ever exactly the same.
We can't deny the ways we change.
I must run toward each moment
and learn to look at earth again,
learn how stars explore what's left them.
Just yesterday the night began to love me.
This morning I noticed how the sun shook loose
in the tall white beeches behind my house.
I welcome those trees, that shaft of light.
I welcome the long enduring night.
I welcome the witch in my elder tree.
A second ago, I heard her
singing, "Bird on my branches,
little brown bird,
look for the fruit in the flower."

SEAL AT STINSON BEACH

She asked brown eyes, "Burn me loose.
Unmask this loss of estuaries, lamp shells."
The lowland wheat dreams against moonlight
and empty houses creak their own tough joy.
On this wintry coast, remember how, in faint light,
Mother's eyes wore green, how
Eleanor sank. A trunk along flat pine.

Beyond breakers, a mute hunter floats, forgetful
of running sharks, sea moss. Teach me
your crisscross answer
to the cackling of gulls,
Closets can mend
sinister days, yet these losses hum
in the walls.

He swam a shadow, a blemish on the waves.
Is this the last year of tasting dust,
of violent wakings?
Blue seashot boils around my shoes. Breakers crash.
Hiss again. He leans, foreign as a star,
for places where the man-of-war
hangs its tendrils down.
In the drawing back, the breathing in, I find my bones.

FOR HEATHER, ENTERING KINDERGARTEN

She tests the curb with a chubby boot,
lolls around the door,
then offers a smile before she walks
down halls that smell of crayon.

When the bell rings, each chart clings
to another from the day before.
Too willing to be wrong, she knows our clock
doesn't tock the same as theirs, and I'm afraid

she'll learn the true length of forlorn,
the quotient of the quick
who claim that snowflakes never speak,
that myths are simply lies.

Aware of each minute and its death,
I scrubbed my Catholic
desk with nubs of tissue and piqued
the sister's early prayers.

Some, bullied into disbelief,
want clues to the terrible cutting
taking place as we race to reason.
I want to gather shreds of bark

and press them in my forehead.
I want to stand near curbs and sing:
The stars can hear. In what season
will you send a message?

Sixth-graders scorn my truth. Heather walks away,
sways in delightful idleness while somewhere
mountains flowers in a sudden gust of wind
openly send word to Algol and Procyon.

Variations for Two Voices

I.

Where do we live?
  Underneath sunset.
How long have we been here?
  Since your grandfather's death
  when war came without effort
  and hearts didn't own
  a tear or a victory.
  We stand in a stranger's field
  beyond pardon.
What do we do?
  We hide. We bargain.
  We answer each question
  with a difficult anger,
  map the future for heartache
  and rattle old bones.
When is it time?
  Time is that beggar
  living in the basement.
  He dictates to us
  when to move, how to dream.
  Run and he'll be there
  waiting at crossroads,
  with pitch for your ribcage
  and pins for your eyes.
Who'll come to save us?
  No one. Nothing.
  Yet when the wind stirs
  I hear voices call us
  inside the snow drift.
  I've heard it those nights
  when snow writhes before Spring.
  Don't ever listen.

Don't ever listen.
Don't listen. What
it can bring!

II.

Where do we live?
  Inside this morning.
How long have we been here?
  Only the lakes remember
  our arrival. Go there at dawn
  when reeds ride the slow wash.
  An answer will come
  from the small world of crayfish.
What do we do?
  Balance our shadows
  like oaks in bright sunlight,
  stretch and tumble
  as much as we're able,
  eat up the light
  and struggle with blindness.
When is it time?
  Time is a thrush
  that preens in the wood
  and sings on a slender branch
  in your ribcage. Listen
  to what comes on invisible wings
  darting above the blue roots
  of flowers. Fly, Dragon
  fly. Now the bird sings.
Who'll come to save us?
  For some, it's the rattling
  cloud, the air before evening.
  Come, take my hand,
  for all that it's worth.
  Our hearts learn
  much too soon
  how to speak like mountain
  stones.

MINOR INVASIONS

It goes, yet isn't gone,
this dust invading my square of sun.
My mother saved her days until she died,
fighting these little boats
that break the monotony of sunlight.
She denied it fell from stars.
She called it dirt and did it in.
The highboy, always hungry for her touch,
swallowed with a blackness not of earth,
a necklace of feathers and cones,
a flower, love letter, favorite Easter egg.
All wasted things belonged in there.
Its dust was all mirage.

Dust knows the value of lost days,
days when do, do, do wrenches
from us too the screech of boxcars.
Memories work against us,
gathering that darkness inside the eye,
until winter roars its final white.
Now I let go, struggle with these moments
brought like waves, and feel them break
as soon as they are formed.
I let the long drawer of the past
swallow once again
the old photographs in whose relentless light
we both stood
without a speck of dust.

LOVE, THE FINAL HEALER

for Jacob

We unstuck a walking stick walking
down a wall and shoved it in a jar
where it hung, a crooked finger.
You slept through the night
while I had the nightmare:
It snuck out through an airhole
and grew to a kitten's size.
I felt its suction feet smacking
up my arm and woke to see
a tree limb with shrewd eyes
arch its back over half my life.
Son, we've little time and much to learn.

The April you were nine months old
a meadowlark in the cottonwood near Mission
forgot her name
and courageously sang at three a.m.
Birdsong in darkness rippling my world
beyond reservation borders and the Nebraska line,
I went out to find her
above the scraps of snow
and came back, fully alive,
to dishes greying in the sink. I wanted
to be happy, but the screen tore and curled,
the nails cried in the walls,
the heater failed, and winter blustered back,
stronger than before.

Scared and hot, you fussed for hours
in the light of a motel,
too dark to be a home, too full of unknown noise.
We're caught in some old story.

I'm the woman winter loved
and you, the son of winter, ask
where did he go and why.
This poem gets cut to just one sentence:
You grow old enough and I get wise.
Yes, the days ride stallions
and leave us in the dust,
yet the details of these days
must imply a different ending.

When we drove through Minnesota, your toes
ate summer air. On an Oklahoma hill,
we poked a puffball with a stick.
Its spore vanished into blackjacks,
a forest just your size.
In Riverton, Wyoming, I wouldn't buy that rock,
bland as the staring rancher in the Teton Coffee Shop.
We could fly to Equador. Customs there differ.
Families are so big and poor that fathers pray
for just one wife. Instead let's accept
the hallways we've walked
toward a winter ripe with ozone,
toward changing drifts of flowers.

What can I teach you that the sun
doesn't show, caring for the sky?
He puts on cloud pajamas, returns with bird
and early blue. What rhythms do I know
that would match water? When it chants,
the frogs and fish experience the world as one.
The wind reveals far more tricks
as you cartwheel in the semi-dark
under a half-moon and your favorite star.
I can only whisper what I'm learning still,
what the trees completely understand.

After every turn of innocence and loss,
in the awful stillnesses to come,
when we give what's true and deep,
from the original in ourselves,
love, the final healer, makes certain
that we grow. A bug, a bird, a phrase
from some old story or a friend will find us.
Then we'll remember winter as a cleansing,
like a note held high and long
above a vast terrain. As we walk,
we'll see the yellow butterflies
lighting on the alfalfa, working on the wind.

IV. Music for Two Guitars

MUSIC FOR TWO GUITARS

for Ernie

I don't have words to mark what clings to me.
　　All day I've been fastened to the sky.
A streak of sun weaves together the bare woods
　　Out my window, while I dream over coffee
I've kissed you, quietly as wind wakes an early garden.
　　All day I've been fastened to the sky.

The hawk, perched twice above his acre, didn't care
　　How we flew through the nourishing dusk.
Purple clouds gathered in mountains; more snow
　　Carries life to those summits in Spring.
Curled near your heart, I'll stay in dark foothills.
　　We, too, have leaped lightly such sad, dismal things.

What a beautiful wing, this blindness
　　Born of delayed elation. My body throbs.
You have robbed my hesitation and distrust.
　　You have taken my fears and wrapped them in fires.
Full of possibilities, I cannot name what rings me.
　　Bell or empty bowl? Guitars on the verge of song.

A Song For What Never Arrives

We aren't like those who kiss like fishes,
lightly, easily, quickly gone. Let's sink
entwined to those reaches
beyond this human world, where tongues
of ripples form familiar kinship.
Inside me, summer leaves have begun
a meditation, and I wake from dreams

as one might wake from fever,
bewildered by the smoke billowing
from my neighbor's chimney. When the vacant sapphire
sky finds an alley of black trees,
I feel you haunt an unknown layer
of my heart. How can I set in order this debris?
It's all I am.

Charmed by illusion,
by nature consistently cruel and kind,
born to confusion,
perhaps we shouldn't plan to arrive at the end
of love, but should move inside its mystery
like chickadees, those acrobats darting in and
out of branches, paled by frost.

Perhaps it's best we accept the thrum of water alone.
Like weeds, we grow submerged in shadows,
feeding on the last fire of a stone.
Yet we can emerge from our lagoon
so tangled up that children,
reaching for one tinted bloom,
will gather both blazing quietly as stars.

REACHING NEW TOWN, N.D.

I had planned to touch you
like wind over water,
one light change of color,
my hip, that shadow of ripples playing
where no boat had ever been,
until at last you'd sing in sunlight
while waves tipped with foam
headed toward shore.

I thought you would touch me
like wind through cottonwoods,
every limb, every leaf, rustling and churning,
until at last that sunrise
until its one leaf still trembling
while the warblers in my blood
key, key, key their happy questions.

We were neither wave nor wood,
but wind finding wind in North Dakota.
The marsh grass knew and waved us on.
Lake Sakajawea stirred dark those three days
until funnels formed in the sky over Stanley.
Wind over wind. I dreamed of tornadoes
and welcomed their voices,
my love, oh, my love.

Dream of Rebirth

We stand on the edge of wounds, hugging canned meat,
waiting for owls to come grind
nightsmell in our ears. Over fields,
darkness has been rumbling. Crows gather.
Our luxuries are hatred. Grief. Worn-out hands
carry the pale remains of forgotten murders.
If I could only lull or change this slow hunger,
this midnight swollen four hundred years.

Groping within us are cries yet unheard.
We are born with cobwebs in our mouths
bleeding with prophecies.
Yet within this interior, a spirit kindles
moonlight glittering deep into the sea.
These seeds take root in the hush
of dusk. Songs, a thin echo, heal the salted marsh,
and yield visions untrembling in our grip.

I dreamed an absolute silence birds had fled.
The sun, a meager hope, again was sacred.
We need to be purified by fury.
Once more eagles will restore our prayers.
We'll forget the strangeness of your pity.
Some will anoint the graves with pollen.
Some of us may wake unashamed.
Some will rise that clear morning like the swallows.

PATTERNS

If I could track you down to have you taste
the strawberry shaded by beggar's green,
the winter wheat, remote as sunlight
through low-moving clouds, we'd face
the squash blossom, fixed in its quiet temple,
and breathe in rhythm to our own beginnings.

Instead I step without your echo
over the cucumbers' tapestry of tendril
and wooly stem. The corn, my blind children,
mingle with wind and I walk naked
into their midst to let them brush my hips
with searching fingers, their cuffs alive with rain.

When I ask if they are happy,
a few by the fence whisper "Yes." It comes
through the rows, yes again
and again yes. My feet take root
in rings of corn light; the green earth
shouts more green against the weighted sky,

and under poppies of ash, patterns emerge:
lilacs collecting dark beneath the sheen of elms,
cedar buds tinting air with memories of frost,
a tanager's cry deep inside the wind break,
my life's moiré of years. When my jailors,
these brief words, fumble with their bony keys,

I listen to the arguments of flies, to the long
drawn-out call of doves, for lessons in endurance.
Moths, twilight in their wings, dance above the oatleaf,
and I know you stand above the same muted sea,
brooding over smoke that breaks
around hollyhock's uneven pinnacles.

For a moment, we are together,
where salt-stunted trees glory in the sun, where verbena
and jasmine light the wind with clean tomorrows.
I felt us there, felt myself and not-myself there.
We lived those promises ridiculed in solemn days.
We lived with a hunger only solitude can afford.

CLIMBING GANNETT

While you clambered up ahead,
jabbing a staff into chunks of snow,
I rested on a rock shelf, wedded
to my breath, to ridges and plateaus,
careening blue and bluer,
to aspens below, flickering
in a downhill draft.

Lengthening its hollows,
the teal blue peak above us
made you laugh. Never did you feel
as close as then,
straddling the distant slope,
balancing in cold wind.
As you climbed beyond my help,

a rim of the crevasse broke to foam.
I heard your wild echo.
"It's no storm." When the mountain
hurled boulders across the sky,
your face blazed in the close grey air,
then the slide pulled you
with a roar, whirring loud

and long, like the wingbeats
of a hundred hawks. Although I held on,
my life leapt at your glance.
I held on for weeks, for weeks I walked
the crumbling fields. In the homeland
of ravens, I stroked the shadow
of each gangling pine, and measured

the distance to your grave.
Across the vista, other peaks darkened.
You were swept away so suddenly.

Surely you'll tap,
perhaps below that copper ridge,
or in that far ravine,
I dream on the icy plain.

Nameless and alone, I sang
in the yellow light of a lily,
and woke to welcome you,
bound by a miniature range.
Outside our window, a warbler claims
another dawn. Do you think
the light drove away that colder wind?

MADE OF MIST

I stumbled on each step as I went down
to hear the water, rumbling on my left,
to see the rocks, creating a shelf
with bright colors streaked in red and brown.

Isolated in a big, black rubber coat,
I heard the wind, but could
the wind hear me, sitting aft
and singing as the boat

dropped from dock and churned on churning waves?
Warm sun and mist rolled over every face.
Lovers locked their elbows and changed place.
I walked along the rail. The engine slaved

along the falls, ferns hiding a lair
where a snake lay twisted into stone.
Tomorrow, even this, a darkened wound.
A thousand gulls charmed that frantic air

and I have never felt that kind of love.
Lost in wing beat,
in heavy spray, wanting to meet
their frail lament, I moved

to the front where motion bound with praise
was the whole world,
and I have yet to stop being swirled
through the dark and light of coming days.

MOTHER

Once I tried to build you out of boxes,
but none had the proper warmth
and I can't remember how you lugged
laundry to the line or tied your apron.
I was the one who watched you sob
in rhythm with the treadle,
the needle traveling over the tweed
for my new coat.

You drugged me so I'd sleep all night,
but still I wandered down
that deep blue sleeve to your room,
crawled between you and Dad
where a garden grew under mothsoft blankets.
Chinaberry trees bathed me in green
while phlox and windflower
leaned into my life. There,
too, the guinea hens of your stories
hunkered in the dirt.

Tucking mothballs in the blankets
one morning, you found silence heaped
behind winter coats in the closet.
Quivering, you kept this to yourself,
but grew more optimistic as you died,
planning rides in the park,
the next picnic, and frequently telling us
we'd like the way
Spanish moss trembles in acacia trees
when we travel south.

Tiptoeing down the hall, we found
a translucent shell curled
in your sheets. Attendants took you
to a cleaner room, rendered your shape

a channel for sunlight. Mother,
your mouth was always pursed
slightly open as you slept.
Between drunken ghosts,
I've listened to that bell for years.
Tempered by your trembling chin,
your hot last kiss,
I knew at nine
that love and death were equal
and that no one was left
to whip such notions
from my unforgiving hide.

WOMAN SEED PLAYER

for Oscar Howe

You balanced her within a cyclone
and I believe the young wind
that frequents the graveyard
tugs her sleeve. Her hand never wavers,
though the stakes are always high.

When running shadow turns rattler,
her concern is how the mountain rises
beyond its line of sorrow. Then,
shooting her seeds, she bids
the swallow fly over rolling hills.

I have been obsessed with permanence.
Struggling in that space under every word,
I've heard exuberant waves drift
denying limitations. Last April
when we trudged upstairs

to where we found you sketching,
you said no one had ever gone full circle,
from passion through pattern and back again
toward pebbles moist with moonlight.
How easily the rain cross-stitches

a flower on the screen, quickly
pulls the threads, varying the line.
Many times this year, I've watched that player
play. She doesn't force the day
to fit her expectations.

Now she pulls me through.
The leaf light dust and her stable hand
allow my will its corner of quiet.

Watch dust embracing the nervous wheat;
every throw's a different combination.

Dust whirs brighter in the door jam,
one last uproar before the rain.
Her bundle contains and yet foregoes
the dark dust already fallen for tomorrow
from long-since gentle stars.

from a picture by Oscar Howe

LYNN POINT TRAIL

That rare day we played for real
and left traces of our walking sticks
in last year's leaves. Lynn Point Trail
hid us in rushing green, in the quick
dark of douglas fir where death conceals
itself in blazing moss.

Leading us in the journey,
our children stomp-danced until the ferns
bristled with the authority
of hooded cobras. When they turned
to us for answers, we began to see
fronds tremble with a delicate weight,

as if infinity had stirred the stem.
The scattered light peopled each ravine.
We longed for woods this deep, for this glen
where you knelt to photograph a gleam
inside a bridge of stone. Was it then
Missy wouldn't go on?

Our youngest girl wanted to believe
home could be this emerald grotto.
Nearby, we heard the breaking sigh of waves,
while, bickering in a bird's staccato,
she kept her gesture firm, though naive:
Here we belonged.

A cuckoo's call echoed in the sun.
I, too, wish we could have lived
near the tilted horizon,
close to the fluttering mat that weaves
dun fly and dune into one.

With songs for granite and bluer skies,
children gathered rain-eroded shells.
Let these rocks be eggs until the tides
scorch them, or until the heart reveals
at last the grace we lost.

GLOSSARY

Star Quilt - Plains Indian women make quilts with a central star for their children and grandchildren. A young man seeking a vision may take one to use during that time. Some are also used as blankets. In either case, it is a valued possession, connecting the generations to one another and to the earth.

Coyote - An ancient trickster figure, he portrays our human capacity for cruelty, deception, ignorance and lust, although sometimes he surprisingly and often unknowingly is beneficent.

Mosquito - A figure who appears in several Oneida stories, he is usually a giant no one can control. As he fixed supper one night, my father told me how people came from the blood of a hacked-up mosquito. He explained that when mosquitoes took a bite, they were only taking back a little of what they gave. I've never heard that story again, although I learned there were others. My father loved to tease.

Longhouse - Traditional homes of the "Hau de no sau nee," they are structures that symbolize the League and the people's natural relationship to the earth.

Cybis - a manufacturer of porcelain.

I'uni kwi athi? hiatho - father's name. He never told us what it meant.

Stone throwers - a band of "elves" who live in caves near the water.

Porcupine, South Dakota - One of the towns close to Wounded Knee on the Pine Ridge Reservation.

Minneconjous - One of the seven divisions of the Lakota Nation, which translated means "Those Who Plant by the Stream."

Stinson Beach - A beach north of San Francisco on the California coast.

Algol and Procyon - Algol, a variable star in Andromeda dims and brightens every two days. Procyon in the Little Dog Constellation is our sun's neighbor.

Gannett - the highest peak in Wyoming, southwest of the Wind River Reservation.

Roberta Hill Whiteman grew up around Oneida and Green Bay, Wisconsin, earned a B.A. from the University of Wisconsin and an M.F.A. from the University of Montana. She has participated in several Poets-in-the-Schools Programs throughout the country, including Minnesota, Arizona, Wyoming, South Dakota, Oklahoma, Montana and Wisconsin. Her poems have appeared in anthologies and magazines, including *American Poetry Review, The Nation, North American Review, A Book of Women Poets from Antiquity to Now, Carriers of the Dream Wheel,* and *The Third Woman: Third World Women Writers in America.* A member of the Oneida Tribe, she has taught at Oneida, Wisconsin; Rosebud, South Dakota; and, most currently, the University of Wisconsin–Eau Claire. In 1980, she married Ernest Whiteman, an Arapaho Artist who illustrated this collection. Together, they have three children: Jacob, Heather and Melissa.